Into the Interior

First published in the United Kingdom in 2022 by
Shearsman Books
P.O. Box 4239
Swindon
SN3 9FN

Shearsman Books Ltd Registered Office
30–31 St. James Place, Mangotsfield, Bristol BS16 9JB
(this address not for correspondence)

www.shearsman.com

ISBN 978-1-84861-845-9

ACKNOWLEDGEMENTS
With thanks to Jonathan Minton, editor of *Word For/Word* #38
which first published Alan Halsey's eight poems and pictures
from *Into the Interior*.

Into the Interior

Kelvin Corcoran
&
Alan Halsey

Shearsman Books

The travellers met the two-headed dog
trained to keep eyes on
near & middle distance
& in particular the fearful horizon.

Alan I've been out to Parc Malou
a cold morning of it along the track
through the devastated trees after the storm
nothing but dogs and corvids in possession.

Kyiv is burning and I sit here dumb
looking into the interior unmapped;
to see your mind at play is everything
in the toytown tangle of fearful horizon.

One told the other he remembered
one of those signs from long ago
& he thought it had something to do
with a keyword in Christian lingo.

The no way-in no way-out catechism
as formless as jelly in the lexicon of splat;
fly little birds, pay no heed to pain,
the centre is hollow and stringman is dancing.

It's no labyrinth, my lords are not that smart,
and will suffer silver bullets of rain like the rest of us:
dance stringman, check your memory,
its certain resonance stands unbound.

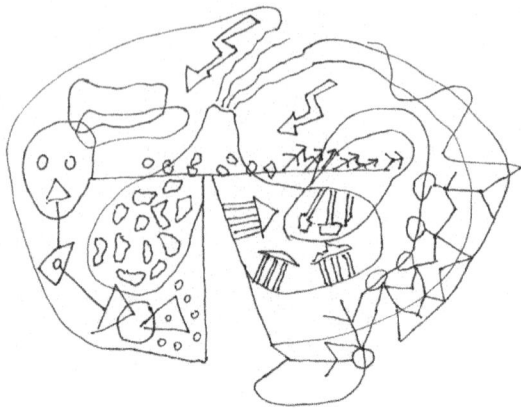

This must be the world turned
upside down on their maps
they'd certainly been warned
a world in imminent collapse.

The world's gone tapsalteerie O
said the one head-down on the frontline.
And what part of your mind, your mouth
are you using to come out with that? – said the others.

This is what it's like under the volcano,
all the temples of Arcadia drawn in one breath,
lightning and dogfish fill the sky, a forest of arrows
heading out of the frame off-kilter.

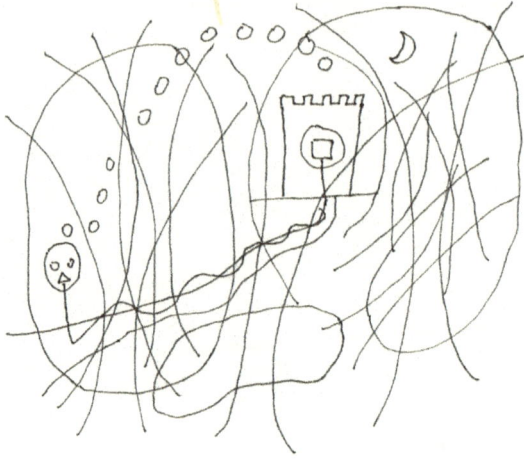

O Pilgrim Pilgrim
there's a dark wood in dreamland
& the tower to which Childe Roland
O Pilgrim Pilgrim

Childe Roland to the dark tower came
to find a window ablaze and the process of thought itself.
Alan, this is just a way of talking to you;
Childe Roland, admirer of spontaneous architecture.

Pilgrim pilgrim, stretching the lines of speculation,
the slip of moon above the dark wood dreams,
the trees sway as one, the oak, the beech, the ash;
and the way through is just a feature of composition.

Beware the lunar eclipse
when spiral flowers bloom
& who knows whom
midnight thunder claps.

Q If the elements conspire
   and flora spirals, what of the morning
   bright and chill after the temporary moon
   and your face away on a kite?

A At the centre is a secret mechanism
   hidden below the one true mappa mundi;
   there every country is joined and shaken
   and every moment in the storm recalled.

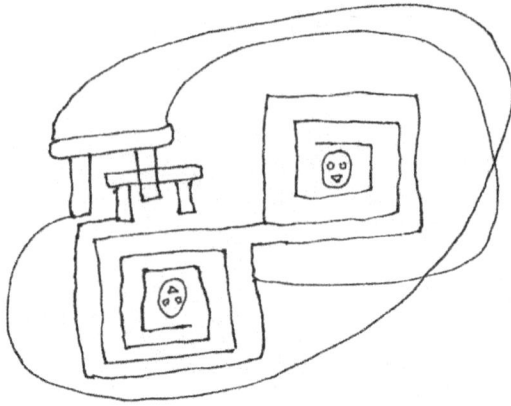

What it was to be
doubly welcome
what it was to be
unkindly undone.

I am bound for the see-saw world again.
Can you pull me through this window?
Can you scout the maze perpetual?
It is only my face staring out – mute.

Boxy you, boxy me, I've had enough.
Somewhere out there the perfect abstract art
loops and dances articulating everything,
shredding graphite like nobody's business.

There it stood
the Great E
the remnant letter
of Exist or Exits.

It has taken 5 steps to get here
to the centre of the leafy riot,
a capital place of some delight.
I make it 96 leaves in this arbour, approximately,
allowing something for degraded print
and the ambiguity of image.
I count two faces certainly, allowing for nothing,
I see there's no escape in the wild wood.

Let's go home says one
Where's home asks the other
If you know which way
you're out on your own.

I remember home but not going to it,
a river runs below a hill, fields, other pastoral features;
there the weather touched my face
and she lay back in the grass.

Go on then, take me home, wherever that is.
Somewhere here in this picture implied,
somewhere between these thinking dots,
the conspiring trees and house of stars.